The Adventures of Charlie Mac to the Arctic and Back

For Charlie, my greatest adventure yet.

In school sat Charles MacDoodle, Charlie Mac for short.
He was Ms. McNeil's favorite and first in every sport.
But when the school bell rang and his friends ran to play,
Charlie sat and dreamed of places far away.

That very afternoon he was in for a surprise.
"Today we'll take a field trip!" sang Ms. McNeil with pride.

Inside there was a theater with a screen that touched the sky,
where they wore special glasses to see creatures passing by.
Bears sparred and whales spun and birds filled the air.
When the credits rolled, Charlie couldn't leave his chair.

This great northern land was a vast exciting place,
where he dreamed all night of going to meet the animals
face to face.

So early the next morning,
while the house was sound asleep;
Charlie tip-tip-toed
and left without a peep.

Soon his footsteps crunched with snow,
a bite was in the air.
The smells of earth and whirling winds
whispered he was there.

Across the bright horizon
shone a furry coat of white;
as the boy approached
he saw a bear... to his delight!
Yet inching even closer,
a sadness filled the air.
"What's wrong?" Charlie asked
of the little polar bear.

"Years ago at this time bears fished out at sea,
hunting seals from ice floes catching two and sometimes three.
But temperatures are rising, and ice is slow to freeze,"
explained the polar bear stretching out on his knees.

"When ice floes don't form, bears have less and less to eat.
Catching seals without ice is a difficult feat.
So we sit and we wait and we find kelp to munch.
If you weren't so friendly I'd eat you for lunch!"

Then Charlie left the bear,
and headed for the sea;
he had much to explore
and many animals to meet.

Once wrapped in a wet suit he stepped from the land,
into dark and salty waters, his camera in his hand.
Submerging into frigid blue unsure of what he'd see;
when out of nowhere came a whale... two and three!

They were white as the snow,
kind of chubby and cute.
Swimming up all together
in a welcoming salute.

He followed the belugas,
  as they danced through the waters,
    taking photos of a walrus
      and some charming little otters.

Then one whale turned and fled
shooing two and three away.
"Orca!" they chirped,
and dashed across the bay.

This underwater boss
takes his pick for dinner...
and breakfast, lunch and snacks;
he's the watery food chain winner.

Charlie bravely swam closer
to the black and white whale.
"I've never seen a predator
with flukes for a tail."

"Lately," shared the orca, "food's been hard to find.
Pollution in the ocean hurts fish of every kind.
When sea life is destroyed, we all have less to eat.
There's no escaping dirty waters when fish have no feet."
Then Charlie kicked his flippers, thankful for his feet,
but sorry for the sea life with less and less to eat.

His legs began to cramp
so he pulled himself ashore.
After swimming all this way
the land looked different from before.

Sitting down to think
on a spongy bank of land,
the earth felt soft and supple...
like Mother Nature's hand.
His thoughts were interrupted
by a young caribou,
who stooped with budding antlers
that were velvety and new.

"Hello!" greeted Charlie. "Where's the rest of your herd?
Don't you migrate together like fish, whales and birds?"
"As temperatures grow warmer the earth will seldom freeze,
creating mushy marshlands where we sink up to our knees.
This really slows us down, it's tough to stay together.
More caribou are lost each year due to warmer weather."
"Come with me!" Charlie said, and together they embarked.
Sharing stories and exploring, a friendship had sparked.

Then from over the hill,
spread a blanket of brown.
What looked like tiny ants moving
grew in size and in sound.
"Hooray!" cheered the buck,
trotting off toward the herd,
as they stampeded by
like a low-sweeping bird.

As he watched them fly by,
Charlie's thoughts turned to home;
to his mother and father
and the distance he had roamed.

Turning in his tracks he thought, "My parents must be worried.
Did they miss me in school?" Charlie wondered and hurried.
"Yet what of these animals? What of their homes?
With less food to eat and less land to roam.
How can I help them, how can I take a stand?"
Charlie mused as he left from that faraway land.

Straight to City Hall he marched,
upon returning to town;
recruiting Mayor Muldooney
to gather folks around.

Arctic Animals
in Danger

Boy Braves Arctic

Arctic Animals
in Danger

He told them of the ice floes
that are slower to form,
and other arctic changes
due to temperatures warm.

They ran a front-page story in the local Star-Gazette,
featuring his photo and the animals he'd met.

With Ms. McNeil's help he formed a club at school,
making arctic conservation a cause that was cool.

And though they had worried, Charlie's parents were proud.
Reminding, "Traveling alone, son, is not yet allowed!"

CONSERVATION TIPS
FOR KIDS AND FAMILIES:

REDUCE

1. Turn off the lights when you leave a room.
2. Turn off the TV or computer when not in use.
3. Unplug electronics and appliances when not in use.
4. Wash your clothes in cold water.
5. Dress lightly instead of turning up the air conditioner on a hot day.
6. Dress warmly inside your house when it's cold outside instead of turning up the heat.
7. Ride your bike or walk to school instead of asking for a ride.
8. Plant a tree.
9. Take shorter showers.
10. Turn off the water when brushing your teeth.
11. Use energy efficient light bulbs.

REUSE

1. Reuse your shopping bag at the store.
2. Pack your lunch in a reusable box.
3. Use cloth napkins.
4. Use rechargeable batteries.
5. Use refillable pens and pencils.
6. Reuse paper.
7. Call toll-free numbers and ask to be removed from mailing lists.

RECYCLE

1. Separate aluminum, glass, paper and plastic from your trash and recycle.
2. If you don't have a recycling bin, call your city and ask for one.

YOUR VOICE

1. Learn what your local and national representatives are doing about climate change and let them know the issue is important to you. They may have other suggestions for you to help.

YOUR HEART

1. Spend time outside having fun whenever you can. The more you love and appreciate the world outside your home, the more you will be inspired to protect it!

LIKE US AT "ADVENTURES OF CHARLIE MAC" ON FACEBOOK!